Help! My Grandchild Has ADHD!
What This Child and His Parents Wish You Knew

Judy M. Kirzner, M. Ed.

ISBN: -10: 1475064985

ISBN-13: 978-1475064988

DEDICATION

I dedicate this to Charlotte Myerstein Marcus
and Gertie Kirzner,

The GRANDmothers of my children

Contents

Preface

I.	What Does It Look Like	1
II.	Myths and Misconceptions	7
III.	Stress Reducer or Producer?	17
IV.	Impact on the Family	23
V.	Impact on the Marriage	25
VI.	Impact on the Siblings	35
VII.	Grandparent Emotions	41
VIII.	Family Gatherings	47
IX.	The Social Impact of ADHD	51
X.	What About the Future	59
XI.	Famous People of Learning Problems	67
XII.	The Special Bond Between You	81
XIII.	Even More Ideas!	95
	Notes, Resources & Index	105

In appreciation to Janet Chahrour who got me started,
My husband, Jerry, who helped me at every step, and
Gale Klayman who gave me the final push!

Preface

Grandparents, like heroes, are as necessary to a child's growth as vitamins.

~Joyce Allston

For more than twenty-five years, I've worked with children and adults who had been diagnosed with learning disabilities, attention deficit hyperactivity disorder, oppositional defiant disorder, Asperger's syndrome, language disorders, Tourettes syndrome, obsessive-compulsive disorder and a combination of these disorders. Even though my job description was working with the students, a major part of my routine included working with the parents of these children or the spouses of the adults. One characteristic was always palpable in working with them—fear. Yes, sometimes the diagnosed person had feelings of fearfulness, but the fear I experienced most often festered in the parents and close relatives. What kind of things were they afraid of?

- Will he have a normal life? Marriage and family of his own?

- Will he be picked on and bullied because of this?

- Will teachers/coaches/other parents judge him unfavorably?

- Can she succeed academically or have a career?

- Will my parents compare him unfavorably to the other grandkids?

- Will my parents think I caused this? Have I?

- Will I always have to take care of her?

I'd like to share some good news with grandparents of Attention Deficit Hyperactive Disorder children.

1. ADHD children can achieve great successes and fulfillment.

2. ADHD children can learn skills and tools that can enhance the quality of their lives.

3. You, as concerned grandparents, are not alone.

4. You, as a grandparent, can help make it happen!

So many wonderful books and websites can tell you all the science and statistics about ADHD. They provide any specific information you could ever want concerning teaching methods, laws regarding disability rights, brain development, or even summer camps for children with these issues. This book is written with a different purpose in mind. It is written for grandparents. In addition to very basic but necessary facts, you'll find practical suggestions and ideas for becoming the GRANDparent of your very special grandchild.

Just about the time a woman thinks her work is done, she becomes a grandmother.

~Edward H. Dreschnack

Chapter I. What Does It Look Like?

- How do I know my grandchild has ADHD?
- Did my own children exaggerate the symptoms instead of being good disciplinarians?
- What are these symptoms?
- Does it look different at different ages?

What is an attention deficit hyperactivity disorder? By the way, the term ADD has been replaced by ADHD, even if hyperactivity (H) is not present. It is the most commonly diagnosed psychiatric disorder in children affecting 3-5% of children around the world, according to the Center for Disease Control. This means that over four million children have been diagnosed with ADHD and this number continues to grow. It is diagnosed more frequently in boys, probably because girls with ADHD often are not as noticeable. Girls are often more compliant and don't make 'trouble' so they are overlooked. ADHD is chronic—it does not go away. Often times it is hereditary, so think about how you or your own child compare to diagnostic descriptions! These children usually have at least one close relative who also has ADHD. Research has shown that ADHD can be genetic, which means that it is likely that you will notice many behavior similarities in other generations of your family.

Even though the diagnosis involves personal opinions, it is real. It can be controversial. Some people believe it is a diagnosis of convenience—parents cannot manage their child's behavior so let's blame it on something else. I am embarrassed to say I have even heard fellow teachers say that! It is genuine folks, and healthcare professionals recognize it as such. We hear much debate about treatment and medication, but the diagnostic criteria are standardized. There are some common symptoms that the American Psychiatric Association divides into three categories; inattentive, hyperactive impulsive, or a combination of both. Let's look briefly at these descriptions.

Inattentive means difficulty listening or easily distracted. Sometimes these kids are listening, but they are listening to the wrong thing! Maybe they are daydreaming, or maybe they are listening to something going on in the hallway instead of listening to the math lesson. Sometimes these kids ignore the signs in math problems, or have trouble following directions or remembering daily routines. These children may be sitting perfectly still and not causing others to be distracted. Many of these kids go undiagnosed.

The **hyperactive and impulsive** kids are very noticeable to the teachers, families, and other students. These students have a really tough time sitting still. They fidget, get up or squirm in their seats, and don't seem to want to take a nap or sleep soundly at night. The impulsive kids speak out of turn, speak incessantly, seem disorganized, and jump from task to task or topic to topic. They seem to have racing motors and no brakes. We like to say these kids approach life in a 'ready, fire, aim' mode.

The third category **combines both the inattention and the impulsive/hyperactive** symptoms. Okay, you say that everyone has some of these behaviors, but do they occur so often that they significantly interfere with work, school, or personal relationships? How frequent is the behavior? How severe? This is the key.

There is no simple blood test that can diagnose ADHD. When a teacher, parent, or physician suspects ADHD, several people who can observe the child in a variety of situations are asked for input. First, the pediatrician is consulted to rule out medical conditions that might look like an attention problem such as an ear infection or vision problem. Sometimes anxiety or depression look like ADHD. Babysitters and coaches have the opportunity to observe behavior in structured and unstructured activities so they make excellent evaluators. Teachers see another aspect, and parents see another. Several observers are asked to fill out a survey rating the severity and frequency of the following symptoms. Results are compared to the peer behavior expected for various age groups. Again, the frequency and severity of the behavior determines the difference between the norm and the ADHD child.

The DSM-V, The Diagnostic Statistical Manual of Mental Disorders, is a widely used mental health reference book that lists characteristics, descriptions, criteria, and treatment for the diagnosis of mental disorders. It is helpful because it provides a standard way to make a decision and uses common language to describe symptoms. Using their list, weighted by their frequency and severity, a diagnosis can be made. The complete DSM-V criteria for ADHD are listed in the book notes in the back if you'd like to know exactly what it says.

Keep in mind that a behavior that is completely acceptable and in the range of 'normal' for a preschool child may be an indicator of ADHD for a child in the elementary school. Let's look at common signs you might see in different age groups.

Preschoolers might:

Have great difficulty learning numbers or rhyming words

Fall or bump into things frequently. They might have difficulty sitting still or be fearless risk takers

Cry more than others or have other very intense outbursts

School age children might have:

Confusion with left/right, up/down, time concepts

Difficulty with small motor hand activities such as holding a pencil or crayon, using scissors, buttoning, zipping, handwriting, or learning to tie shoes

A hard time sitting down and getting work started, switching activities, or finishing a task

Social group reacting negatively to their inappropriate humor, getting into the other children's space or materials, or frequent clumsiness

Adolescents with ADHD might:

Act impulsively without seeming to think of consequences or engage in risky activities

Have problems managing time, schedules, and activities. Personal things are disorganized—loses items, homework, books, pencils, etc.

Act very socially immature. May misunderstand or misread facial expressions and body language. They might do or say things and not realize the social impact

Get it perfectly one day and do not know it the next day

Remember that each of these behaviors is common in children. The frequency and intensity of the behaviors are the basis for making a diagnosis of ADHD. Also, ADHD is not the same as a learning disability, but they often occur at the same time. Not all children with ADHD will have reading problems, and not all children with a learning disability will have an attention disorder.

Okay, now we know what it looks like. Let's move ahead and become GRANDparents!

Grandma always made you feel she had been waiting to see just you all day and now the day was complete.

~Marcy DeMaree

Chapter II. Myths and Misconceptions about ADHD

- Why are old myths and misconceptions about ADHD so frustrating?

- What kinds of comments upset parents of ADHD children?

- What are some of the most common myths and misconceptions about ADHD?

- How can grandparents help?

A huge cause of frustration for the parents of ADHD children is the numerous myths, misconceptions, and untruths often spread about this disorder. Believe it or not, sometimes it's one of the

7

parents who holds tight to an ADHD myth and contradicts the strategies used by the other parent. When a child's teacher believes these misconceptions, it can be a very uncomfortable situation for the student and for the family who is trying to support their child. When a grandparent believes and perhaps spreads these myths, the situation can result in pain, hurt feelings, damage to the self-esteem of the parents and the child, or even permanent damage to family relationships. I've asked parents of ADHD children for personal remarks about this. These are real comments from the heart; a direct result of hurtful remarks about the myths of ADHD.

Myth #1: Kids with ADHD do not use their inner discipline because their parents don't teach them how. They could behave better if they wanted to. ADHD is a convenient label rather than a real disorder.

"I struggle with the criticism and sad advice everyday. I've gotten it all: the "eye-rolls", the lectures about how I'm too permissive with him or that there's nothing wrong with him. Or my all time favorite: "When we were raising our kids, there was no such thing as ADHD. If you acted up you got spanked. That's all he needs is a good whooping."

"My husband blames me for my five year old's issues. He says I am a bad mother. His family agrees with him."

ADHD is real. It is recognized as a disability under federal legislation (the Rehabilitation Act of 1973; the Americans With Disabilities Act; and the Individuals With Disabilities Education Act). It has been recognized as a disability by the courts, the United States Department of Education, the Office for Civil Rights, the United States Congress, the National Institutes of Health, and all major professional medical, psychiatric, psychological, and educational associations. In fact, federal and state law mandates accommodations for ADHD individuals. These accommodations are in place to level the playing field for these individuals and certainly not only because they have a convenient label.

According to most sources, ADHD is probably "caused by biological factors which influence neurotransmitter activity in certain parts of the brain," and it is very probably strongly genetic. If one person in the family has it, there is as much as a 25-35% chance that another family member also has it. When you compare this to the general population where there is only a 3-5% chance of having it, statistically it seems to be inherited.

Children with ADHD are not misbehaving or distractable because they want to be. They are trying to sit still and pay attention, but it is beyond their control. It is not purposeful disobedience. Dr. Russell Barkley and others have demonstrated that just using more punishment and stricter discipline alone tends to worsen behavior rather than improve it.

It is important to spread the word that ADHD is NOT caused by:

- Poor parenting

- Too much sugar
- Food allergies or food coloring and other additives
- Too many video games or television

Myth #2: Kids with ADHD can never pay attention or finish anything.

.   **"My mother-in-law says her grandson cannot be ADHD because he pays really good attention to TV shows he wants to watch. He is only inattentive when he doesn't feel like paying attention."**

Children with ADHD are often able to concentrate on activities they enjoy. I have heard teachers and parents say that the kids can pay attention when they want to.   Truthfully, they have trouble keeping focus when the task is boring or repetitive. Some kids do better when they multitask, some need to move around or stand up, and some need to have some kind of music or auditory background rhythm. During school instruction, kids often are taught in classrooms while sitting perfectly still or in a completely quiet environment. Teaching styles often use step-by-step thinking, or watching rather than doing. ADHD children need to be actively involved in the learning process. Also, many of them do not learn in a linear fashion. Their minds jump and their thinking shoots off in tangents.

Myth # 3 Kids with ADHD are below average intelligence.

"Here are the facts. . . children with ADHD are not mentally slow. My daughter will be able to finish high school. In fact, she will be able to go to college if that is what she chooses. You have already written her off, like she's going to end up a high school drop out or something. Have faith in my child. Love her and see her strengths. Please look at her and see what she can do, not only the things she cannot do."

ADHD does not impact intelligence. Many ADHD children are extremely bright—probably even in the gifted range. The problem is that ADHD might have a negative impact on the ability to have academic success. They might not be able to apply knowledge or be able to stick to the tasks required to be successful. Also, during intelligence tests, I have observed very intelligent children with creative minds pick the wrong answer to a question because they look at a problem from multiple points of view. I've asked them to explain how they made their answer choices. Their reasoning is incredibly deep and thoughtful—much more than the test creator ever had considered. They were plausible answers, but incorrect on a test with only one 'right' response.

Myth # 4 ADHD children are over medicated.

"What a convenient bunch of baloney. Today's parents do not know how to be disciplinarians, so they make up this problem and give the kids medicine. It's easier to give the kids medicine that dulls their brains than to make them follow some rules and behave.

"It would be really nice if the grandparents were supportive of the situation. My mom believes that I have him medicated because the dr's and teachers cant handle a hyper child. She does not believe in ADHD or ADD. She thinks it just a reason for parents and doctors to put their children on medication and sedate them."

Research has repeatedly shown that children, adolescents, and adults with ADHD benefit from treatment with Ritalin (also known as methylphenidate), which has been safely used for approximately 50 years. There are some negative side effects. Some children complain of appetite loss, and some show some moodiness or "rebound effect" when the Ritalin wears off. In some cases, children will develop temporary tics. Contrary to belief, Ritalin does not alter growth permanently or cause weight loss. Ritalin does not cause Tourette's syndrome, but there are some children with Tourette's who have a comorbid condition of ADHD. Some children who suffer from the tics of Tourette's actually have fewer tics when they take Ritalin, so it often makes even more improvements.

Myth # 5 Girls do not get ADHD.

"My mother-in-law tells me that I need to get tough with my daughter. She says she only acts this way because I let her. She also says that my daughter cannot have ADHD because she's a girl and girls don't get it."

Girls absolutely do get ADHD, but they are sometimes overlooked or diagnosed at a later age because they do not act out like the boys do. They might be described as flaky or spacey. Girls are more likely to have inattentive ADHD, rather than hyperactive. This would cause more problems in staying focused or paying attention, rather than in disrupting the class with outbursts. As they get older, the symptoms become more obvious in social situations. Perhaps they make inappropriate social responses because they cannot keep up with the pace of conversations or read the body language of the other girls. They appear to be insensitive to the situation, when actually they have a problem figuring out what the situation is! Social issues are an important way of discovering that a girl might have ADHD. Also, as the academic load increases in upper grades, the ADHD female might have difficulty organizing all of the materials and assignments required when you begin to change classes and have several different teachers.

Myth # 6   <u>All</u> kids with ADHD are hyperactive. That's why it had the 'H' in it.

> "My mother says it isn't that ADD thing because she can sit still for hours playing with stuff. If anything, she says, she under active and not over active. She is more of a space cadet than anything else."

Even though the ADHD label is the accepted name of the disorder, some children are diagnosed as being the predominantly inattentive type of ADHD. These children have multiple inattentive symptoms, but few hyperactive/impulsive symptoms. These are the children who used to be diagnosed as ADD without hyperactivity. Some children with ADHD truly are hyperactive, but many others with attention problems are not at all what we think of as hyper. Children with ADHD who are inattentive but not hyperactive might seem to be unenthusiastic or unmotivated to do their work. They might look like they are daydreaming.

Myth #7   Kids will eventually grow out of ADHD because ADHD is a childhood problem.

> **"My mother says to skip all the medications, appointments, and IEP meetings. My son is almost in high school, and she is sure he will outgrow his ADHD any day now."**

> " It's really funny. My husband tells me he was just like our son when he was little, and he doesn't have it anymore. He says he grew out of

it. Boy, was he wrong! My husband is just as ADD as ever! He doesn't even realize it!"

ADHD often continues into adulthood, so don't wait for your child to outgrow the problem. Treatment can help your child learn to manage and minimize the symptoms.

Over 70% of children diagnosed as having ADHD will show all the symptoms during their teen years, and 15-50% will continue to suffer from these symptoms as adults. It isn't going to go away. People mature and learn better coping skills, so it appears to have diminished.

Myth # 8   There is really no medical method for diagnosing ADHD so it is a disease of convenience!

" if our kids had some other disability that was more obvious to people, they would not act or say the things that they do. Until they walk in our shoes... they'll not understand."

While there are no physical tests for ADHD, there are diagnostic criteria for determining whether or not a child has ADHD. These are listed in the Diagnostic and Statistical Manual of Mental Disorders (DSM-IV) published by the American Psychiatric Association (1995). A reliable diagnosis can be made by using these criteria and some other methods to collect comprehensive information from several people who are a part of the child's life.

These might include teachers, counselors, daycare providers as well as parents of the child.

What can grandparents do?

How can we correct the damage done by the spreading of false myths? Educated grandparents can educate the rest of the extended family, their friends, and even acquaintances that have misconceptions. Remember, also, that your adult children need your support and acceptance of their parenting. This is a great way to show them you are on their team. By understanding what is true, you will be ready to be a positive force to help others understand.

In summary:

- There are many misunderstandings about ADHD and most of them are negative

- When grandparents do not know the facts, they often make hurtful comments

- When grandparents know the facts, their own patience, tolerance, and helpfulness improve dramatically

- When grandparents learn the facts, they can teach others and advocate for their grandchildren

What children need most are the essentials that grandparents provide in abundance. They give unconditional love, kindness, patience, humor, comfort, lessons in life. And, most importantly, cookies.

~Rudolph Giuliani

Chapter III.   Stress Reducer or Stress Producer?

Do parents of ADHD children have added stress?

Could I, as a grandparent, be adding to this stress?

How can I evaluate my role?

Where can I go from here?

Families of ADHD children have added stress in every part of their daily existence. They feel pressures from each other, their families, and probably their other children. They might be dealing with stresses caused by the neighbors, the school, the community, and from their own feelings of failure, incompetence, guilt, and frustration. They are working with their children with more intensity and longer hours, yet are probably yielding fewer positive results. They might be considered to be lousy parents by their peers, unfair parents by their other children, or indifferent romantic partners by their spouses.

People criticize their parenting skills, avoid socializing with their families, tell them what they are doing wrong, and offer unwanted advise about what they should be doing. Even close family members feel justified in offering their criticism and letting them know exactly what they are doing wrong.

Their ADHD child might feel bullied or unpopular. These children might withdraw, feel hopeless, or become depressed. The kids are fighting battles every day—academic and social—and the parents are sharing this pain to their very core.

When children have visible disabilities, the world has an open heart. Friends and strangers are supportive and understanding. With an invisible disability like ADHD, encouragement comes only from others in the same situation or people who have educated themselves on the topic. The isolation and sense that they must fight the world alone are great stress producers.

Take the following quiz to evaluate your impact as a stress reducer or stress producer. Which side of the scale weighs more heavily for you? If you do not like your results, don't despair! We will use that information to become improved grandparents to our ADHD grandchild.

Are you a part of the problem or a part of the solution? Parents responding to surveys often state these actions by grandparents as being either helpful or hurtful. Read each statement and give yourself a point value. Be honest with yourself in order to grow and improve your stress reducing skills:

0 = Never   1 = Sometimes   2 = Often

Stress Producer

____1. Doubt that ADHD is real

____2. Tell your adult children that all he needs is more discipline

____3. Blame your child's spouse

____4. Compare this child to another grandchild unfavorably

____5. Criticize how the parents handle child rearing

____6. Tell your friends how wild (bad) your grandchild is

____7. Blame this child first when something goes wrong

____8. Expect more from this child than he can give like requiring he sit still for 2-hour church service

____9. Criticize the treatment—such as medication

____10. Refuse to give medication or follow their instructions

____11. Leave valuable breakables around your home and expect nothing to be broken

____12. Blame the teacher or the school in front of your grandchild

____13. Do not try to learn and understand the disorder

____14. Don't see your adult child or grandchild do anything right or good

____15. Openly disapprove of this child so that he worries you will be watching him

____16. Ignore the stress levels and fatigue of your adult children

___17. Point out the imperfections to the child and/or his parents

___18. Feel ashamed by your grandchild, especially in front of your friends

___19. Undermine the parents' rules and schedules because your way is better

___20. Assume that your grandchild will not be a success because of the ADHD

Stress Reducer
___1. Learn everything you can about ADHD

___2. Support your adult child by listening as a sounding board as she vents

___3. Compliment them as parents and let them know you realize how difficult things are

___4. Offer to baby sit or pay for a sitter on occasion

___5. Encourage child's strengths by giving lessons, attending a special program or showing interest

___6. Spend one on one time with each of the children, including their siblings

___7. Offer to do chores, drive the kids somewhere, or do errands

____8. Treat parents to some alone time. Buy movie or theater tickets they would enjoy

____9. Support their treatment options even when you disapprove, as in medication

____10. Promoter of this child's self esteem

____11. Love and enjoy the grandchild unconditionally for who he is

____12. Attend workshops or speakers about ADHD for your own personal growth

____13. Treat your adult child to workshops, speakers, or out of town conferences

____14. Be a safe, discreet sounding board for ADHD children and their siblings

____15. Teach others who have misconceptions about ADHD

____16. Never compare your grandchildren, especially to their parents

____17. Contribute financially to tutoring, special schools, or technology as best you can afford

____18. Prepare a meal or two to stash in their freezer for a tough day.

____19. Childproof your home

____20. Have a special quiet place at your home for the ADHD child for solace, not punishment

Producer _____   Reducer _____   ©2009 JKirzner

The reason grandchildren and grandparents get along so well is that they have a common enemy.

~Sam Levenson

Chapter IV The Effects Of ADHD On The Family

Can ADHD in one child impact the rest of the family?

How are parents affected?

How are the other siblings affected?

What is the impact on grandparents?

An ADHD child in the family will have a huge impact on all family dynamics. As you look at your grandchild, it might seem an exaggeration to say that this invisible disability can flow through the entire family—parents, siblings, the child himself, and extended family members. The analogy that paints the perfect picture is by Rick Lavoie, my favorite speaker and advocate for children with learning disabilities. I heard Rick talk about his workshop called, "On the Waterbed." He told us, "and the reason I call it that is an analogy that I draw that a family of five is like five people lying side by side on a waterbed, whenever one person moves, everyone feels the ripple and that's the way it is in a family. If one member of the family is having trouble everyone feels it."

Just as the child's problems do not only occur in the classroom, the child with the ADHD is not the only family member who feels the pain. At first, there is a period of grieving when the child is diagnosed. Parents and grandparents may have responses such as shock, blame, denial, or guilt. The entire family might feel isolated from others, as if they have to fight the world, hide a secret, or be the only ones they know that have to fight this horrible battle. Siblings are often resentful or jealous. Parents often wonder, "Why us?" All of these feelings are normal, and it is so helpful for grandparents to understand the family dynamics of a rising and falling waterbed. Awareness of what is actually happening will help enormously as you support your children and your children's children. You need to believe that your support is critical.

Grandparents who want to be truly helpful will do well to keep their mouths shut and their opinions to themselves until these are requested.

~T Berry Brazelton

Chapter V. How Does An ADHD Child Affect A Marriage?

Parenting is an exhausting job. No one can argue with that. When one of your grandchildren has ADHD, take that exhaustion, add a lot of stress, sprinkle in some frustration and multiply by five! This is why having an ADHD child will probably put a strain on your adult child's marriage. An article in the *Washington Post* (By SHANKAR VEDANTAM, Posted: Sunday, March 8, 2009) stated:

> "Couples who have a child with attention deficit hyperactivity disorder are nearly twice as likely to divorce or separate as couples who do not have children with the psychiatric disorder, according to a definitive new study that is the first to explicitly explore the question. The reason appears simple: Having a child who is inattentive or hyperactive can be extremely stressful for caregivers and can

exacerbate conflicts, tensions and arguments between parents.

The study, led by psychologists Brian Wymbs and William Pelham and published in 2008 in the Journal of Consulting and Clinical Psychology, longitudinally tracked a large number of families with and without children diagnosed with ADHD . . .

> While 12.6 percent of the parents of children without ADHD were divorced by the time the children were 8 years old, the figure was 22.7 percent for parents of kids with ADHD. Couples with ADHD kids also tended to reach the point of divorce or separation faster."

Pretty scary statistics, for certain. There have been other studies with similar results yielding twice the divorces in marriages with ADHD children. What are the seven most dangerous situations causing this disproportionate rate of divorces in marriages where the children have ADHD?

1. Parents might not act as equal partners in raising an ADHD child

- There is disagreement regarding the diagnosis and/or the treatment of ADHD

- There is disagreement in how to discipline the ADHD child or how much/little to expect from that child

- One parent feels like she or he has an unfair amount of responsibility for child rearing

- Instead of working together, one parent might feel anger or blame toward the other for genetic or any other reasons

2. Communication Problems

- Parents are so overwhelmed with parenting tasks that they are too tired or have no time to talk to each other. Since they have not discussed or reached consensus, they often cannot show a united front on how to handle large or small situations.

- Stress and frustration might cause parents to raise their voices or use defensive, angry language with each other

- Parents might stop talking to each other because it is easier than fighting. Perhaps one parent is frequently absent from the home to avoid the chaos

3. Money Strain

- Special schools, private tutoring, and/or counseling are expensive

- Medication or frequent doctor visits to adjust medication levels might not be completely covered by insurance or might have a large copay

- Technology for ADHD child which is often quite beneficial can be very expensive if the school district does not provide it

4. Alienation/Isolation/ Disconnection

- Other families avoid this family because this child might get into trouble that could draw negative attention or ruin the experience. Adult "friends", as well as other children, do not invite them to join outings that include the ADHD child

- Other parents in the social group and even members of the family look down on them and criticize their ability to parent

- It is easier just to stay home and avoid a possible social disaster.

- It feels like people do not understand what they go through and how much they want to feel 'normal'

5. Exhaustion

- Excessive amount of time is spent on discipline, homework, or any day-to-day activities. Getting the ADHD child through the day just requires more parent input than might be required by another child.

- Survival mode leaves very little personal time which leads to frustration, exhaustion, and eventually depression. A parent simply cannot think clearly under these circumstances

- Exhaustion causes blame and short tempers with spouses, as well as impatience with the children, coworkers, and family.

6. Depression and Self Esteem Problems

- There is a deep sense of loss that their child is not normal and might not achieve what they had hoped for him or her. Parents fear for the future of their ADHD child. Fear uses up a great deal of energy.

- Relying on professionals to help them raise **their** child means that they must be incapable of doing it on their own. Being constantly told how to parent might cause a defensive attitude, loss of self esteem, or resentment toward the spouse or the ADHD child they created.

- Feelings that there must be something personally wrong with them for creating a 'defective' child can destroy confidence and self esteem

7. Intimacy—emotional and sexual

- The amount of time spent on pleasant couple things is diminished. Parents do not have time to laugh or have fun together, or support each other emotionally.

- Anger that builds throughout the parenting hours cannot be turned off. Lack of partnership in parenting roles or philosophy errodes intimacy as well.

- Parents spend all their talk time discussing the ADHD child and his problems. The ADHD child becomes the center of the marriage or the family

- Sex or sleep? No contest for exhausted or pressured parents

- Lack of confidence in parenting often spills over into the bedroom. How can a person love someone else when he's feeling self-loathing?

What can grandparents do to make a difference or even help save an overburdened marriage? I surveyed online parents, asking them what they would like from us as grandparents. The following responses are just a sampling of their replies because the reaction to this question was overwhelming and extremely passionate. <u>This is what they want us to know, but are unable to tell us face to face.</u> Many of these will be difficult for grandparents to hear, but if you really plan to make a difference, this is where it begins. Please read them with an open mind and a warm heart. Maybe you will hear a comment that sounds very close to home. Maybe you will hear something that might just touch you and motivate you in some way:

> We really need a break once in a while if our marriage is going to make it. If you could drive Timmy to tutoring or drive one of the other kids to soccer practice, it would be great! Maybe you could even take one of the kids for a few hours on the weekend. That way we can spend some quality time with the one at home. Or with each other!

I really need your support. Sometimes I feel like I am fighting the world to get my child what she needs. Then, you call and instead of feeling like I have a friend, you challenge me on everything I do, too. I am so tired and I need you to be on my side.

Instead of always telling me what to do, could you ask me what I would like for you to do to help once in a while?

Megan's tutoring is very expensive and it seems to be so helpful. Do you think you could help us pay for some of it? I hate to ask you, but I know you might be able to afford it, or help us add an extra tutoring session now and then. It would be so great if you could just offer instead of putting me in the position of having to ask for money.

Sometimes I just need to hear that I am doing a good job. You were such great parents, and it's tough to live up to that. I have self-doubts sometimes, and it would mean so much to me to hear you say that I am doing a great job and I am a good parent.

Be my cheerleader! Listen to what I have to say without thinking I want you to fix it. I just need to vent sometimes. My whole world was turned upside down when I found out about the ADHD. Please listen and support me. Don't judge me. Don't judge my child. Don't judge my parenting or my marriage. Stay close but give me space. Confusing, huh?

Cut me some slack, mom. I spend hours each night helping with homework, anxiety, and organization. I cannot help it if my house isn't the cleanest. Maybe you could help me clean. Maybe you could get me some cleaning help. I am doing the best I can.

Stop blaming my spouse for your ADHD grandchild! It does not help anyone if we blame a specific person for this problem that is probably hereditary. Yes, we know it is, but does it really matter who gave it to him? Maybe it was YOU!

Mom and mother-in-law--please let me know you are interested. Would you be willing to go along with me to hear a speaker on ADHD, or read a book that I would like for you to read? Maybe then you could understand and support the things we are trying to do.

Please support our decisions, even when you don't agree with what we do. We have asked many experts, talked to doctors and teachers, and spent a great deal of time making these decisions. It is not helpful when you criticize or put doubts in our minds. This is so hard. Please do not make it even harder.

Stop making me doubt myself about medicating my child. I feel insecure about my parenting as it is, and your doubts about what we are doing make me feel even worse. Don't ask your doctor or your friends about my child's medication. If you have specific questions, ask me. Don't talk to my husband behind my back.

Do not talk to all your friends about my child's problems. It's none of their business, and I don't like those looks of pity every time I run into someone from your bridge club! Besides, they end up telling their adult children all about my child's problems, and then everyone is expecting the worst from us before they even meet us! We feel even more like alienated freaks or failures.

Instead of ringing your hands and feeling sorry for yourself because your grandson is not perfect and you cannot brag about him to all your canasta ladies, we know what you can

do! Give us some help, here. Give us some
of your time. Listen to our hearts, learn
everything you can about ADHD, and love
us all unconditionally.

Okay, grandparents. The ball is in your court.

Children need love, especially when they do not deserve it.

~Harold Hulbert

Chapter VI. Impact on Siblings

What are the most common concerns for non-ADHD siblings?

How can grandparents improve the lives of siblings of ADHD kids?

Having a sibling with ADHD has a significant impact on the non-ADHD brothers and sisters. Ages of the siblings, severity of the ADHD, and sex of the children will shape the experience, but there are five common pervasive threads. If grandparents are aware of these feelings, they are empowered to provide support.

1. Jealousy and Resentment

In almost every ADHD family, parents spend more time, more energy, more money, and more of their patience on the ADHD child. These children often require engaged hands-on help with homework. They require supplementary supervision to get ready for school in the morning. Often, a considerable part of the family budget goes toward expenses for tutors, special equipment, medication, counseling, and/or camps. Parents are sometimes worn out from using a large amount of their energy on the ADHD children and have nothing left to give the siblings who can "take care of things on their own." Siblings might get the feeling that the household revolves around the ADHD child. Siblings might even wonder why this has happened to them and why they don't have a 'normal' brother or sister with whom he can hang out with or play in a normal way. They feel that they must adhere to stricter rules and expectations than their ADHD sib. This is a recipe for jealousy and resentment. Some non-ADHD siblings are very confused by these feelings, knowing they are supposed to be a loving family member.

2. Embarrassment

The non-ADHD sibling lives in dread of humiliation by his sibling. An ADHD brother might interfere in phone calls or with visiting friends much more often than a typical sibling. He probably doesn't read the signs that he is unwelcome or uninvited. In fact, siblings will avoid inviting friends to their homes because the threat of embarrassment is always looming. The non-ADHD child might be anxious that people will stare or think poorly of his family during family outings. Wild actions or outbursts in public places or in school are always a possibility. Children are uncomfortable when their family appears different or when extra attention is focused on them. Adolescents are especially apprehensive that they might be disgraced just to be in the proximity of a situation that might draw attention. Some are aware that their family is not included in some outings because other families avoid their ADHD siblings.

3. Guilt

The natural response to being embarrassed about your ADHD brother or sister is guilt. The sibling feels guilty that he is ashamed of his brother or sister when he's supposed to love him. He feels guilty that he resents the extra time and money, because deep down he knows that this sibling really needs the extra support. And, he feels guilty that he does not have ADHD knowing how difficult it makes his sibling's life.

Interestingly, because some non-ADHD siblings feel guilty about their parents have so much added stress, they bury their own needs to avoid burdening them with more. They worry about their parents and try to protect them. They might become perfectionists, or might turn the guilt and anxiety inward. Both of these reactions are unhealthy.

4. Fear

On occasion a non-ADHD sibling feels fearful when the ADHD child is verbally or physically aggressive. The non-ADHD child becomes a victim, never feeling safe in his own home. When parents downplay the physical aggression of the ADHD child, the other siblings live in fright and uncertainty. It also creates anxiety when the ADHD child's aggressive behavior is unpredictable. This is an extremely unhealthy household.

5. Feelings of Being Devalued

Non-ADHD children often feel that their achievements are not recognized or are downplayed. Parents just expect them to be able to do things successfully without parental intervention, or parents do not want to celebrate these accomplishments in front of the ADHD child. Good grades and successes are expected. To make matters worse, parents ask the 'short-changed' siblings to 'give in' more often, be more helpful, be more forgiving, or take more care of their ADHD brother or sister than normally expected. They are expected to be playmates, supervise, protect, include, and keep their sibling out of trouble! Imagine how difficult it is for these siblings to be expected to give more, be more, and do more for this person who it appears is already getting the lion's share. Often non-ADHD sibs are left out of discussions and do not understand all the dynamics of their situation. They experience the feeling that something is wrong, yet no one has explained the truth. It is no surprise that non-ADHD siblings often feel devalued and invisible.

What can grandparents do?

Just becoming aware of the range of emotions and dynamics between/among siblings is a first step in helping them cope. Let's see how we can be part of the solution.

1. Realize that each child in the family really needs some one-on-one time with a loving adult. Spend private time with each child, even if it's only a talk while you are driving to the grocery.

2. Really listen to your non-ADHD grandchildren. Be a safe ear that will listen as he complains, questions, shares his feelings about his situation. Try to discourage name-calling and do not rush in to defend the ADHD child, but be sure he is not a victim of his ADHD sib. Do not judge since his perspective is his reality.

3. Help all the grandchildren look for the strengths in each other.

4. Do not punish all the children for the actions of the ADHD child.

5. Do not be overprotective of the ADHD child, but remember that ADHD is not an excuse to ignore the rules. The other siblings will see it as favoritism if you let him 'get away' with too much.

6. Let the children settle their battles unless someone is in danger. Do not referee each skirmish! Remind the grandchildren that it's normal for all brothers and sisters to fight.

It is easier to build strong children than to repair broken men.

~Frederick Douglass

Chapter VII. How does ADHD Affect Grandparents?

As grandparents, it is our nature to worry about the entire family. Let's take some time to pay attention to the effect that an ADHD grandchild will have on us. Every grandparent will not experience all of these emotions, but we are certain to have some of these feelings. Also, I cannot hope to list every emotion that's been experienced. However, it's good to know that your feelings are normal and if you are willing to learn and grow, the scary emotions will not be permanent.

Normal Feelings You Might Experience

Fear—will he be okay? Will he have a normal life?

Disappointment—I wanted a normal grandchild with bragging rights

Confusion—What am I supposed to do? This is all new and I don't understand.

Sadness—Why can't everything be normal?

Anger—This is not fair. I resent this situation. Sometimes I am filled with rage!

Resentment—Why do my friends have grandchildren without these problems?

Shock—How did this happen to my perfect grandchild? It cannot be true!

Defensiveness—It's not from my side of the family! There's nothing wrong with him!

Helplessness—I cannot make this better. He will always have troubles.

Isolation—I cannot tell my friends about this. I am the only one with this problem.

Embarrassment—My grandchild cannot behave/get good grades/ be the star. What will my friends think?

Critical—My daughter-in-law is not a very good mother. She feeds them junk/let's them run wild/doesn't make them behave.

Guilty—I feel bad that I don't want to have my friends be around my grandchild. How can I feel pride in this wild child? I know I'm supposed to feel pride!

Blame—My son-in-law is the cause—my grandchild acts just like his dad! They do not discipline him.

Worry—What if he cannot finish high school? What if he has no friends?

Frustration—If my adult children would just do it the way I did, the kids would be fine!

Doubtful—I don't think these young parents know what they're doing.

Skeptical—I think that ADHD is a convenient diagnosis for kids who misbehave.

Disrespected—My adult children do not value my advice, yet they listen to some shrink!

Ignored—I know how to raise great kids, but my adult children do not listen to me.

Old fashioned—Why don't they just give him a good swat in the behind?

Out of step—I do not believe in 'time out' or medication. I want to roll my eyes!

Unrealistic—Why can't he just sit still? Children can be taught to sit no matter how long.

Jealousy—Why do other grandchildren get good grades? Behave? Stay out of trouble?

Annoyed—Why does every family event have to revolve around this child?

Abnormal—I just want a normal family, normal grandchildren, a normal life!

Uncertainty—What should I say or do that won't do permanent emotional damage?

Sneaky—When the grandchildren are with me, I will do it my way!

Dishonest—If I do not tell my friends about the ADHD, no one will know.

Stressed—I feel on edge whenever I take my grandchild out somewhere!

Wouldn't it be great to feel these feelings most of the time?

Positive—I know my grandchild will grow up to be a productive adult

Helpful—I will pick the siblings up from swim lessons or baby sit

Confident—I know how to teach him about going to the library.

Informed—I have read all about those medications.

Connected—There is a group to share ADHD experiences and I can join

Proud—I share my grandchild's artwork/ideas/special qualities to others

Understanding—I know why he said that. He did not mean to be rude.

Patient—If I let him do it himself, he will learn more even though it takes so long.

Respected—My children know I understand the situation and am doing my best

Consulted—They ask me what I think

Trusted—My adult children know I will follow their rules

With it—I understand the language of ADHD and I know great strategies

Honest—I explain ADHD to others and correct misunderstandings

Normal—I know that normal means accept what you have

Problem solver—I can figure out more than one way to get the job done!

Knowledgeable—I read the research and attend speakers on ADHD

Creative—I plan activities and special outings with my grandchild

Supportive—I do what I can to help and I give my adult children encouragement

Proactive—I plan ahead to be sure things will go more smoothly

An hour with your grandchildren can make you feel young again. Anything longer than that, and you start to age quickly.

~Gene Perret

Chapter VIII. Family Gatherings—A Grandparent's Fantasy

Family gatherings—a time of warm and fuzzy memories of good times and boundless love! This is most likely not the case for parents of ADHD children! Children with ADHD function best when activities and schedules are predictable and familiar. They depend on people and places being the way they are supposed to be. Parents work hard to provide a calm environment and consistent actions, rules, and agendas. Bring on the family gatherings and it can all fly out the window. When the family gathers for special occasions or to celebrate the holidays, the ADHD child, his parents, his siblings, and his extended family all might experience intensified stress and social pressures.

Consider the feelings of the parents, for instance. Parents are going to want their children to act right and make them feel proud. It's the old sibling rivalry rising up from childhood! Each adult child wants to look good to his siblings and his parents. Each wants his children to shine and wants his parenting skills to be respected by the others. So, what if your child is going to be the one with the behavior problems, the one who is aggressive with the cousins, or the one who is loud, or the one who breaks grandma's favorite vase? What if your child hurts your Aunt Mildred's feelings because he tells her she is fat, or he tells her that her Christmas gift is for babies and he doesn't like it? What if your child is so besieged by the increase in sugar, extended bedtimes, or general holiday chaos that he breaks into tears several times a day?

Some parents are so overwhelmed or upset by the possibility of what can go wrong or memories from past disasters that they opt out of important family get-togethers. That is really sad for everyone—the cousins, the grandparents, the parents, and especially for the ADHD children who benefit from social interactions with the family. The parents might feel that it is easier to avoid this stress and save themselves some unpleasant memories or embarrassment. Parents I've questioned are very hurt by family disapproval or to unkind comments from members of their extended families. Listen to just a few of the comments from parents I've surveyed:

> Several family members have taken it upon themselves to correct my children. I try to put myself in their shoes and see that they are only trying to protect their child, but at the same time I think they see my children as the complete and total blame. I'll hear some family members fussing at my children and ignoring others that were

clearly involved. I ALWAYS have to have my eye out for the kids and what is happening,etc.It is so exhausting for me.

My mother-in-law is so afraid that he is going to break something that she hovers over him like you do when your toddler is learning how to walk. Grandma is always asking him what he's doing and where he's going. I am walking on eggshells the entire time.

My brother gets all sarcastic with my son when he does something that my brother thinks is wrong. My ADHD son doesn't understand sarcasm and the behavior just spirals. For example, my brother says something like, "That's just great, and why don't you use even more ketchup on your hot dog?" My son doesn't understand the message and assumes his uncle thinks it is just great. So guess what, he uses more ketchup. Then his uncle thinks my boy is being rude and disrespectful. The tension continues to escalate and my boy is clueless about why his uncle is so mad at him!

Okay, so what can grandparents do to make the family get-togethers better?

1. Prepare yourself, your grandchild, and your household for the visit. This takes planning. Look at pictures together and refresh memories with a bit of information on rarely seen family, and remind her how people are related. Explain what things are going to happen during the visit.

2. Put away your breakable treasures so there is no danger of damage. This is important for all of you. You cannot believe how much stress is reduced by taking time to do this.

3. Limit the number of people invited or shorten the party. Remember not to have every moment of the visit planned. Build in rest time/calming activities as well as time to use large muscles to work off energy!

4. Catch your grandchild doing something right and praise her for it! Give her any role that will let her shine like helping with the meal, joining in a service project, or passing out gifts.

5. Praise your adult children for something you see in their parenting skills. They are probably nervous about their child's behavior and are likely to feel extra sensitive or defensive. Apologize when you interfered or gave unsolicited advice, and support the limits and schedules they've set. Do not sabotage or undermine their rules! Provide some break time for the parents so they get some relief from the stress.

You can never guarantee that things will be perfect when your extended family gets together, but these five tips will definitely be a positive start!

A grandmother is a little bit parent, a little bit teacher, and a little bit best friend.

~**Author Unknown**

Chapter IX The Social Impact of ADHD

Can a grandparent impact a child's ability to make friends or be socially accepted?

What can grandparents do to help our grandchildren with conversational skills to blend in?

Many times ADHD children have social problems. There are lots of children with ADHD who do not have social difficulties, but since it is such a common issue, we will talk about some of the potential problems here because there are so many excellent activities you can use to make a difference. If the child does have social difficulties, this is so very hard on the parents; in fact, this is harder to face than the academic problems. It is painful to hear that you child is unhappy or shunned by other kids. You can be sure that they are experiencing academic and social minefields all day long. Many times, they lose the battles on both fronts. These 'failures' affect their health and well being, even if things are going smoothly at home. Most likely, because of the nature of the ADHD child, things are not smooth and easy at home, either. In fact, if ADHD children have the choice between getting good grades and being popular with peers, almost all of them would choose popularity! The school is not the only place where socially unacceptable behavior would have an impact. These children have problems playing with other kids in the neighborhood, going out to dinner with the family, belonging to a sports team or a scout troop, attending religious services, and even visiting relatives or grandparents. When ADHD symptoms exist, they impact every waking moment of that child's life. This means there is a spillover on parents, neighbors, coaches, siblings, and extended family.

Because the social aspects of the child's life are so important, we need to understand why an ADHD child does what he does. Remember, these symptoms explain the behavior, but they do not excuse it. Let's try to understand what causes the problems and then what we grandparents can do to be helpful.

The impulsivity factor of ADHD means that a child will say or do something without considering the consequences. He does not wait his turn to speak or to take his turn during activities. Instead of thinking or talking through a problem, he might become intolerant and react aggressively. He might blurt out a rude or hurtful comment or perhaps lie to be heard.

The inattention factor might cause him to misinterpret the body language or mood of other people. Because the ADHD child misses details or tone of the language, he might misunderstand what has been said or the objective of the speaker. This results in inappropriate responses or actions. His peers or adults in authority are naturally annoyed and think the child is deliberately difficult.

Do any of these behaviors sound familiar to you? These are a few of the traits that often cause peers and adults to become irritated. The important thing to remember is that the behavior is not something they can control. They are not done with the intention of driving everyone crazy. Your grandchild will probably come to you with some inadequate social skills. Parents of ADHD children frequently report that social problems play an exceptionally large part in their child's day-to-day life. You are not the parent, but you can use your time together to help teach and practice some of these skills.

The best way to develop social skills is to practice them with peers. The sooner this training is started, the more successful the intervention is likely to be. Unfortunately, because of their social mistakes and reputations for them, other children and their parents do not include the ADHD child in the very activities that could help them improve. Even in their own homes, these children cause havoc in day to day living. Siblings might be embarrassed about bringing friends over to play. Parents might be anxious about being judged by other parents and family members. The family might even be excluded from activities and outings because people do not want to risk having 'that ADHD kid' spoil things. Think about the pain this causes the entire family. Ouch!

According to Richard Lavoie in his book, *It's So Much Work To Be Your Friend,* "social skills are the ultimate determining factor in the child's future success, happiness, and acceptance." That is very powerful. We all want to insure the future success and happiness of our grandchildren. While most children learn how to get along by observing, these children cannot. They must have direct and planned social instruction. Grandparents can help!

Social Conversation = Social Success

An important part of successful social interactions is the ability to converse. The ADHD child needs to learn acceptable ways to let others know his opinions and needs while he listens to theirs. Pragmatic language is essential in successfully solving conflicts and maintaining friendships. There is a rhythm and partnership to social language that an ADHD child might not be able to follow. This is easy and natural for most of us, but it is an extremely complex activity for these kids. Problems arise because the listener is distractible or forgets what has been said already. The flow is disrupted and uneven when the impulsive child interrupts or hogs the conversation or veers off in a completely unrelated topic. Casually observe your grandchild during a social conversation. Do you see any of these?

As a speaker

- Talks non-stop or does not let the other person have a turn

- Uses unsuitable volume or tone for the situation

- Uses words or topics that are inappropriate for the setting

- Does not maintain eye contact or use correct facial expressions or gestures

- Responses are off topic or do not follow

As a listener

- Interrupts so he won't forget what he wants to say—often ignoring the speaker's remark

- Stands too close in the speaker's personal space or too far away

- Ignores body language or tone of the speaker

- Does not understand sarcasm or get the joke

- Smiles when hearing sad news or other inappropriate affect

How can grandparents help improve social conversation skills?

Are you willing to spend enjoyable one-on-one time practicing these skills? You are the perfect person to model good listening competence without becoming preachy! Talk about your day to demonstrate what kinds of events a person might mention. Ask her to listen to what you say and think of a follow-up question or two. When she tells you something, stop what you are doing and model the good listening skills you would like her to have. Give her 100% attention and call attention to the way you show you are listening; make eye contact, nod your head, make comments like, "Really?" or "Wow!" and ask questions about something that has been said. Explain that eye contact shows caring, confidence, understanding, and respect for the speaker while lack of eye contact implies disinterest, disrespect, or insincerity. Be sure you put these terms in age appropriate language. When you two are talking, stop speaking if your grandchild stops making eye contact. Make it like a game and keep it light and fun!

Help her prepare a script for an upcoming conversation with another family member or neighbor and then rehearse or role play what she will say while you pretend to be that other person. She can practice necessary dialog and tone to ask permission or express feelings appropriately.

It's really fun to say the same phrase in a variety of moods, i.e. "Pass the pickles." Can you imagine how "pass the pickles" will sound in a frightened mood? Talk about the way the tone changes the message—even with the exact same words. You will probably have to demonstrate and evaluate these together. It works really well while watching yourselves in a mirror. You two will probably be rolling with laughter in no time!

Do you enjoy people watching? You can make a detective game of it at the mall or bus stop. Together you can try to figure out their mood, what they might be saying to each other, how they feel about each other, or how they might be related or connected to each other. Stay out of voice range so this stays private and you don't offend anyone. This is really fun and you can play even if you only have a few minutes! You can work on social skills without leaving home, too. Watch TV together without the sound and try to figure out what's happening using nonverbal hints like expressions and gestures. Charades are also great for interpreting nonverbal language, too.

If you are lucky enough to have your grandchild with you frequently, you might establish a signal to let the child know if she needs to adjust something in her conversation such as volume, eye contact, or topic. Be sure to do this privately and in advance. It could be something like tugging an ear or holding up a finger. Don't do this with the grandchild you see only a few times a year. It could spoil your precious time together.

Remember that by doing some of these activities, you are directly teaching your grandchildren techniques that smooth the way for social acceptance. Our ADHD grandchildren need this direct instruction. It does not come naturally in many cases.

A mother becomes a true grandmother the day she stops noticing the terrible things her children do because she is so enchanted with the wonderful things her grandchildren do.

~Lois Wyse

Chapter X. What about the future?

Is there anything positive about having ADHD?

Do children with ADHD have a chance for a normal future?

What are some of these positive qualities found in ADHD kids?

So often, we talk about all the problems and difficulties that our ADHD children and grandchildren encounter. Let's just put those aside for now and spend some time looking at the positive side of Attention Deficit Hyperactive Disorder. Yes—there really is another side to this coin. Here is what two of the experts say:

> "Several elements of the ADD mind favor creativity....As mentioned earlier, the term 'attention deficit' is a misnomer. It is a matter of attention inconsistency. While it is true that the ADD mind wanders when not engaged, it is also the case that the ADD mind fastens on to its subject fiercely when it is engaged. A child with ADD may sit for hours meticulously putting together a model airplane." - *Edward Hallowell, M.D., and John Ratey, M.D., "Driven to Distraction."*

There are lots of qualities that you love and admire in your grandchild. Maybe you think that your unconditional love is the reason. Guess what, people who work with and observe children and adults with ADHD have noted that there are some very positive traits that seem to be part of the ADHD personality and brain. First, as you already know, these people are very intelligent. True, sometimes schoolwork is difficult or unexciting for them, but it isn't because they are not smart. It's because of some of the other issues that we won't talk about here. This chapter is all about the good news!

Many children with ADHD seem to have a very high energy level. They like to be doing something and seem to have boundless ability to keep on going. These people would much rather be doing something other than just sitting in front of a television. This means they can work hard for a longer period of time. When you spend a lot of time exploring and doing, you are much more likely to experience a wider variety of interests.

This leads to another positive quality, flexibility. ADHD children are willing to switch gears and changing routine is second nature. They are happy to multi-task and consider new ways of doing a task. A flexible person is easy to be with. They go with the flow (and sometimes beyond) and enthusiastically offer unique alternatives.

ADHD children and adults often have very creative minds. Maybe it's because their brains seem to be moving more quickly than the average person. They think outside the box and consider more than one way to do something. These children are often able to see the small details that the rest of us overlook. Their minds move in many directions, often not in a straight line. They may daydream and tie these dreams together in ways that the rest of us do not. They explore and ask questions—sometimes at the wrong time! I remember talking to my class about the novel *Treasure Island* while looking at a map of the route from England. An ADHD 6th grader raised his hand (this is good!) and announced that his family had made a trip to one of the small Caribbean islands that was barely visible on our map. This was not unusual for him. He leaped from paying attention to the discussion to an understanding that the other children hadn't yet reached. His brain was skipping from the large treasure map to tiny details. His mind bounded to thoughts of sand, bugs, seasickness, sunburn, palm trees, and the moist heat of the islands. He remembered these feelings from his family cruise. His comments and understanding of some of Jim's difficulties along the way made the novel a richer experience. By personalizing it, he understood the novel in a way that most of the others had not. If I hadn't known about the way his thinking could spider web, I might have thought he was being rude and disrespectful. He wasn't inattentive; he was thinking faster than the others. This tangential thinking made his insights much richer than most of the other students.

Sometimes creativity is in the arts, and sometimes in the sciences, but either way it's a very powerful trait. Hearing the music that others haven't heard, or seeing a scene and painting it in a way that others haven't imagined are the gifts of a creative mind. How could you ever invent a tool or solve a problem if your mind was incapable of thinking outside the box? If your thinking goes only in a straight line and you do things in the way they have always been done, you will never invent a better mousetrap. Our ADHD children and adults can combine their creativity, flexibility, and incredible energy to find a way.

Many ADHD children are risk takers. True, this could be dangerous, but nothing changes without taking a risk. Their impulsivity causes them to act before considering all the possible outcomes. Most of us avoid risks because we think too much about what can go wrong. Maybe we could have created or engaged in something life changing if we had been willing to take a risk. In this particular chapter, we will say that risk taking is a positive quality and necessary for growth and creativity. What if????

Still another positive quality is spontaneity. Who doesn't like to be around a fun person who is always thinking of new things to do and ways to do them? Someone who doesn't dwell on the consequences? These children are lively and entertaining, so take time to enjoy this gift.

Darcy Andries, the author of the ADHD section of the website www.suite101.com, has created a positive list to share. She has worked as a special education teacher, an ADD/ADHD coach, and has been diagnosed with ADHD herself. As you read a limited number from her list, I encourage you to think about which of these you find in your own grandchild! In her article, she says,

"Here are just a few traits that are more prevalent in people with ADHD. Not everyone who has ADHD has all these traits, and sure people who aren't ADHD have these traits too. . ."

1. Sensitive, Compassionate, and Forgiving
2. Charismatic, outgoing, and personable
3. Intuitive (when you miss out on stuff because you're distracted, you learn to figure things out)
4. Imaginative & Innovative
5. Flexible, Resourceful, and Hardworking
6. Humorous and fun loving
7. Humble (it's not hard when people are always telling you what's wrong with you)
8. Observant (it seems like inattention, but it often is over attention)
9. Takes risks (sometimes this can be good)
10. Passionate &Tenacious

"I advise everyone who is, or knows of someone who is, ADHD to print this list to keep it handy for those times you forget what a blessing being ADHD can be."

Darcy Andries, Writer

In summary

- Experts have documented that ADHD children often have a unique set of behavior qualities
- The combination of high energy, creativity, and spontaneity are a powerful force
- Embrace these qualities rather than wishing your grandchild would act just like everybody else. Unwrap this gift!

- College, relationships, marriage, and success are the norm and not the exception.

So, grandparent, share their passion and enthusiasm, partner in their spontaneous activities, and indulge their creative brains. You never know what the results will be. Take a look in the next chapter to see where these qualities just might take your grandchild!

We worry about what a child will become tomorrow, yet we forget that he is someone today.

~Stacia Tauscher

Chapter XI. Famous and Successful ADHD Individuals

What does the future hold?

Is there a limit to her future potential?

How can some of those positive traits help?

Grandparents are natural worriers! So, we want to know if our ADHD grandchild has a chance for success in life. Without a doubt, the answer is yes! These children can have satisfying careers, attend good colleges, and have happy marriages. Want proof?   These ADHD success stories should make grandparents, parents, and especially your grandchildren hopeful about their possibilities.

Take a minute to scan these lists.   Our ADHD students can be great in many fields. This is not a complete list of all the individuals who have succeeded. Although they had ADHD attributes, all were not formally diagnosed with ADHD.   There are people from every profession, race, nationality, and background who have learned how to adapt and draw on their differences. These people are just the ones we know about, but let's not forget scores of unknown doctors, lawyers, teachers, and others who have struggled and made it.

Why were they able to make it? ADHD people have unique gifts!   They tend to be creative, imaginative, resourceful, and think outside the box. This is where new ideas come from--brains that are always on the go. Many of these famous people had great difficulty with the rigid expectations of the typical school day, but that surely didn't stop them from making their marks on the world.

Grandparents—read this list, share it with your grandchildren and their parents, take a deep breath, and realize that your grandkids have a very bright future! All is well.

Actors and Musicians

Bill Cosby	Jim Carey	Jack Nickolson
Cher	Kirk Douglas	Ann Bancroft
Dustin Hoffman	Robin Williams	Suzanne Somers
George Burns	Steve McQueen	Tom Cruise
George C. Scott	Sylvester Stallone	Whoopi Goldberg
Henry Winkler	Will Smith	Stephen Spielberg
James Stewart	Tom Smothers	Mozart
Elvis Presley	Joss Stone	Alfred Hitchcock
Jay Leno	Woody Harrelson	Jewel
Patrick Dempsey	Tony Bennett	Beethoven
Joan Rivers	John Lennon	Keira Knightley
Rachmaninov	John Denver	Harry Belefonte

Artists

Salvidore Dali	Walt Disney	Tolstoy
Edgar Allan Poe	DaVinci	August Rodin
Lewis Carroll	Agatha Christie	Robert Frost
Pablo Picasso	Vincent Van Gogh	Ansel Adams

Athletes

Bruce Jenner	Pete Rose	Magic Johnson
Jackie Stewart	Babe Ruth	Michael Jordan
Nolan Ryan	Jason Kidd	Greg Louganis
Evel Knievel	Terry Bradshaw	Michael Phelps

Inventors

Leonardo Da Vinci	Orville & Wilber Wright	Benjamin Franklin
Thomas Edison	William Wrigley	Alexander Graham Bell
Sir Isaac Newton	Galileo	Albert Einstein
Henry Ford	Bill Gates	Werner von Braun

Leaders & Politicians

Anwar Sadat	Abraham Lincoln	John F. Kennedy
Winston Churchill	Prince Charles	Dwight Eisenhauer
Robert F. Kennedy	Woodrow Wilson	Nelson Rockefeller
General Schwarzkopf	Napoleon	Alexander the Great
Ben Franklin	Nasser	General Wm. Westmoreland

Entrepreneurs

Walt Disney	FW Woolworth	Andrew Carnegie
Henry Ford	Malcolm Forbes	William Randolph Hearst
Bill Gates	Tommy Hilfiger	John D. Rockefeller
Milton Hershey	Frank Lloyd Wright	

Many of these people will tell us that the road to success wasn't always easy. In fact, for many of these individuals, school was a very unpleasant time of life. It is encouraging to our grandchildren to hear that some of these people were feeling exactly the way they are feeling right now. For example, Thomas Edison's teachers told him he was too stupid to learn anything. "My teachers say I'm addled . . . my father thought I was stupid, and I almost decided I must be a dunce." -Thomas Edison "I remember that I was never able to get along at school. I was always at the foot of the class." - Thomas Edison

Sir Isaac Newton did poorly in grade school! His teachers felt he wasted too much time trying to 'make contraptions.' They described him as "idle" and "inattentive." His achievements and ideas, however, still have impact on the scientific world. He is noted for his work in gravity, motion, calculus, the first refracting telescope, white light and the color spectrum, a Member of Parliament, and religious writings and interpretations. So much for his lackluster showing in grade school!

Albert Einstein is often mentioned in the list of misunderstood learning disabled all stars. Albert Einstein did not speak until he was four years old and could not read until he was seven years old. Hans Albert Einstein, talking about his father stated, "He told me that his teachers reported that . . . he was mentally slow, unsociable, and adrift forever in his foolish dreams."

The great poet, Robert Frost, was expelled from school for chronic daydreaming. A newspaper fired the wonderfully creative Walt Disney when his editor said Walt had "no good ideas." Can you imagine that?

Winston Churchill had academic and social troubles in school. "I was, on the whole, considerably discouraged by my school days. It was not pleasant to feel oneself so completely outclassed and left behind at the beginning of the race." - Winston Churchill

Do you enjoy a good Agatha Christie mystery? Here's what she said about herself: "I, myself, was always recognized . . . as the "slow one" in the family. It was quite true, and I knew it and accepted it. Writing and spelling were always terribly difficult for me. My letters were without originality. I was . . . an extraordinarily bad speller and have remained so until this day." - Agatha Christie

Many of your grandkids wear Tommy Hilfiger clothes. This is what this popular designer had to say about his education. "I performed poorly at school, when I attended, that is, and was perceived as stupid because of my dyslexia. I still have trouble reading. I have to concentrate very hard at going left to right, left to right, otherwise my eye just wanders to the bottom of the page."   When people recalled Tommy as the class clown, he said: "I didn't want anyone to know that I didn't get it." We see this behavior over and over. Children prefer the negative attention of being a bad boy to attention from appearing stupid.

Whoopi Goldberg "remembers being called dumb and stupid because she had a lot of problems reading." She recalls that she didn't think she was stupid, but she didn't understand why she was having school problems. Our grandkids look up to Magic Johnson, but he laments, "The looks, the stares, the giggles...I wanted to show everybody that I could do better and also that I could read."

Stephen J. Cannell is a screenwriter, producer, director, and novel writer: In interviews he said several notable things.

"Since I was the stupidest kid in my class, it never occurred to me to try and be perfect, so I've always been happy as a writer just to entertain myself. That's an easier place to start. I am somebody who had a horrible academic experience and came out of that to be successful"

Here is a great one to share with your discouraged grandchild!

"Failure in school does not mean failure in life." - Stephen J. Cannell

Remember the Fonz from *Happy Days*? Here is what Henry Winkler, the Fonz, had to say about himself. "When I was in the fourth grade, my self-esteem was down around my ankles. And I couldn't read. It's still difficult for me to spell, to do math, so I

74

always thought it was important to help young people understand that they were great just the way they were. Self-esteem is the beginning and the end of living." –

Henry Winkler, in a *USA Today* article said it this way. "School was this immovable object," he recalls. "I was told I wasn't living up to my potential, that I was stupid. My parents, being short Germans, were convinced I was merely lazy. So I was grounded for most of my life. I did not see the moon during my junior year. When you are in the bottom of the class, you're constantly feeling less-than. You're always working overtime to achieve some sort of normalcy or cool factor, which I had none of." He certainly was very cool on *Happy Days!*

Anthony Hopkins, the famous award-winning actor, still has memories of his father's fear that he "was not like other boys."

Hopkins said, "I think children can be very cruel especially in adolescence and if you are slow, and I was (I was in a school which was quite competitive) you do get a lot of slamming about from the other kids. I don't know about girls, but I know that boys are very cruel and very tough. It built up a tremendous resentment in me because I was also bad at sport and athletics and all I could do was play the piano. So I always got the sense in my adolescent years that

'Oh, Hopkins, you know he's, well he's not worth much, or he's a failure." - Anthony Hopkins

Beautiful, talented singer and actress Cher confesses, "I never read in school. I got really bad grades--D's and F's and C's in some classes, and A's and B's in other classes. In the second week of the 11th grade, I just quit. When I was in school, it was really difficult. Almost everything I learned, I had to learn by listening. My report cards always said that I was not living up to my potential."

Hearing that over and over is enough to make anyone want to quit!

Tom Cruise is another famous Hollywood celebrity who willingly tells about his school struggles. He had great difficulty learning how to read, and managed to keep this his personal secret for many years.

Tom said, "I'd try to concentrate on what I was reading, then I'd get to the end of the page and have very little memory of anything I'd read. I would go blank, feel anxious, nervous, bored, frustrated, dumb. I would get angry. My legs would actually hurt when I was studying. My head ached."

Most recently, our ADHD hero is record setting gold medal winning Michael Phelps. Deborah Phelps, mother of Michael recalls, "He was always full of energy. He'd talk constantly, and ask questions nonstop. He also had trouble focusing in school, and his teachers said they couldn't get him to interact during learning time. He was always pushing, nudging, shoving, and fidgeting. It was hard for him to listen unless it was something that really captivated his attention, so you can imagine what bedtime was like!" Some say that Michael is great because of his ability to have complete focus on his swimming. Marie Paxson, board president of CHADD (Children and Adults with Attention Deficit/Hyperactivity Disorder) says, "Phelps's success demonstrates that being a part of a supportive family, setting goals, engaging in enjoyable activities, and receiving positive feedback, are all important in building self-esteem. Phelps is clearly an exceptionally talented athlete and a source of pride for the millions of people affected by ADHD.

Have you ever heard of Kinko's? Who hasn't? The man who started Kinko's was diagnosed dyslexic and ADHD. His name is Paul Orfalea, nicknamed Kinko because of his curly red hair, and he started his business based on his own coping tools. He needed lots of copies. The other students needed copies, too. He found a way to supply these copies at a cheaper price. Voila! Kinko's is born. "Building an entirely new sort of business from a single Xerox copy machine...gave me the life the world seemed determined to deny me when I was younger."

Paul says that he had a difficult time in school. He was held back in elementary school, and he scraped the bottom in high school. His college grades weren't much better—lots of C's and D's. He describes himself as ADD to the max! Orfalea's parents were extremely supportive, however. "Kids with dyslexia and ADHD can develop a brutal self-image if parents reinforce society's negative labels and make them feel inferior to others," he says.

"With ADD, you're curious. Your eyes believe what they see. Your ears believe what others say. I learned to trust my eyes." Orfalea. "My biggest advantage is that I don't get bogged down in the details, because of my ADD. I hire capable people to handle that."

Sally Shaywitz, pediatrics professor and researcher at Yale School of Medicine explains it this way, "People with dyslexia often have outstanding thinking and reasoning skills and an impressive talent for conceptualizing and creative thinking. Similarly, the restlessness of ADHD can be a motivator for action, and the curiosity and adventurousness it brings can propel entrepreneurs to take bold chances and ignore naysayers in developing truly unique products and services."

David Neeleman is another enterprener who claims that his disability was the key to his successful Jet Blue airline. He is crediting his ADHD for his ability to think outside the box. "With the disorganization, procrastination, inability to focus, and all the other bad things that come with ADD, there also come creativity and the ability to take risks," he explains.

Alan Meckler, Chairman and CEO of Jupitermedia, attributes his business success to his ADHD. "My lack of concentration, my inability to read charts, and my difficulty in deciphering documents made me a much better business person," says Meckler, 59. "And my lack of patience forced me to cut to the chase. I'd just find my mind wandering off," recalls Meckler, who had problems with standardized tests. "I wasn't able to spend much time on something if I couldn't come up with the answer right away." This internet mogul was certain he had a "math block."

"What we need is for children to know with the right help and right work, not only can they be just as good as others, they can excel," says Dr. Edward M. Hallowell. Be sure to share these names and their stories with your grandchildren. Help them see that there are good days ahead. Encourage them to use their special ways of thinking about things to change the world.

In summary

- ADHD children do have bright futures!
- Many ADHD adults owe their success to their ability to compensate and solve their own problems.
- Many ADHD adults owe their success to the very behaviors that caused some of their academic and social problems .
- Grades and classroom performance are very weak predictors of future success

- Sharing these struggles and success stories with your grandchild and with their parents can be a very positive and helpful activity. They might just provide a connection and inspiration.

If you want your children to improve, let them overhear the nice things you say about them to others.

~Haim Ginott

Chapter XII. Your Special Bond as a grandparent

- How can I develop a special bond with my grandchild?

- Can I make a true difference in his chances for success?

- What can I do to bond with my grandchild, build his self-esteem, and impact his future?

Grandparents have a unique gift to give their ADHD grandchild. It does not cost any money, and it appears instinctively the moment they hold that baby in their arms—unconditional love. It conveys a willing heart, complete acceptance, and the message that they will always be in his corner. It says that they love this child for who he is and not just for what he will be able to do. It says, "I love you, no matter what!" Unconditional love is the essential base for the construction of self-esteem. Children can recognize this special emotion that comes so naturally to a grandparent and they can feel this special bond.

Self-esteem can mean the difference between having a successful life and becoming a failure. Does that statement sound too significant? It cannot be said too often. It's true, and grandparents have the power to influence this difference. Self-esteem affects the way a child feels about his image, his thoughts, his abilities, and his value as a human being. Strong self-esteem leads to confidence, a positive attitude, a sense of pride, and even happiness. A child with good self-esteem is better able to deal with mistakes, balance friendships, and persevere. It is the report card he gives to himself. A child with low self-esteem might feel powerless, of little worth, and be easily influenced by unsavory adults or peers. He might become withdrawn or even depressed. So you see, development of self-esteem really is a powerful responsibility! ADHD children have a tendency toward problems with self-esteem, especially when their ADHD affects academic success. It's really difficult to feel good about yourself when almost every day you have a social problem, a school problem, or both. Imagine getting pounded over and over with negative messages. We cannot hold his hand at school, but the feelings we develop when we are together can carry him a long way. What can grandparents do to enhance a child's self-esteem?

The Coordinated Campaign for Learning Disabilities (CCLD) is a collaborative effort of many national special education organizations to share public awareness and information about a variety of disabilities. Dr. Robert Brooks, noted speaker on family relations and motivation, has collaborated with the CCLD to provide a list of ten suggestions to help parents raise children with strong self-esteem. Let's use that list as a starting point and borrow the ideas that apply to grandparents as well.

1. ## Help your child feel special and appreciated.

    Why is this important? There is actual research showing that if a child has even one adult who can make him feel special and focus on his strengths instead of his weaknesses, that child can become more resilient when problems do occur. It gives a child hope, confidence, and a feeling that he matters.

    What can grandparents do to help?

    - Set aside special one-on-one time doing something he likes to do and give him your undivided attention. Ignore your cell phone and other preventable interruptions.

    - Learn more about a subject he is interested in. This shows you care, as well as you value his interests. Ask questions that show you want to know more about his ideas. It also gives you something special to share.

    - Be certain that any praise you give is honest and accurate. He will know if it is not deserved.

2. **Help your child develop problem solving and decision making skills.**

Why is this important? Children who can problem solve feel better about themselves because they have a feeling of being in control of their world. This feels empowering. It is also associated with high self-esteem.

What can grandparents do to help?

- Take the time to discuss a few possible solutions when a grandchild has a social or logistic problem. If he can't think of any solutions, suggest a few and talk about what might happen in each situation.

- Role-play one or two possibilities that you have come up with together. Don't feel silly—really try to act it out! This is excellent practice for the ADHD child.

- Model your thinking aloud so your grandchild can hear you strategize. 'If I say this, how would Billy respond? Would he like the idea, or would he get mad about it?"

- Next time you are together, find out if the plan or decision was a good one. Try to figure out why it did or didn't work.

3. **Avoid comments that are judgmental and instead, frame them in more positive terms.**

   Why is this important? Telling him to try harder makes it seems like you think he isn't trying. If a child is doing the best he can do, it is discouraging to hear the people he loves tell him that he should do it better. It feels defeating and hopeless. It makes a person want to give up since it feels like nothing is going to work, anyway. It chips away at confidence and self-esteem.

   What can grandparents do to help?

   • Acknowledge the hard work and effort that you observed. Praise the strategies that worked well so they can be reinforced and utilized again some time.

   • Have an upbeat attitude to show that you are not discouraged or ready to give up. Show your confidence that there is more than one way to do something. This models tenacity, problem solving, positive thinking and acceptance of differences among people.

4. **Be an empathetic parent.**

   Why is this important? Letting children know that you appreciate their effort and feel their frustration for their disappointments helps you form a partnership rather than becoming a judge. When children feel they have to defend themselves, they feel unsupported and perhaps even unloved. Having an understanding adult in your corner is comforting and helps reduce the stress that destroys self-esteem.

What can grandparents do to help?

- Let him know you understand his problem and are willing to help him figure out what to do about it. Be available when you are asked. What a special honor!

- Be a safe confidant. Let your grandchild vent about his problems or frustrations without becoming critical or passing judgment.

- Listen rather than jumping in to fix or suggest a solution. This is a very difficult thing to do. Grandparents want to make everything better or make it go away. It is more important to brainstorm ideas that will help him solve the problem. If *you* solve the problem, you not only take away the grandchild's opportunity to build this skill, you also give him that message that he is not capable of handling things by himself.

- Correct his inaccurate opinions of himself. For example, if he says he is a lousy student, you might say, "You do have a difficult time with spelling, but you are really good at writing creative stories."

5. **Provide choices.**

   Why is this important? Making choices gives the ADHD child an opportunity to take control of some pieces of their day. It feels empowering and builds independence. These are important traits of strong self-esteem. Even if the choices are small ones, putting some control in the hands of the ADHD child increases his ability to make decisions and take responsibility. Putting some decisions into the ADHD child's hands demonstrates your trust in his opinion and abilities. This technique will also help with smoother discipline as offering a choice is less confrontational than issuing a command.

   What can grandparents do to help?

   - Offer two options for many of your day-to-day activities. For example, "Would you prefer Sloppy Joes or grilled hamburgers tonight?" or "Would you prefer to brush your teeth now or after we read a story?"

6. **Do not compare siblings**. Never, never! Can this EVER have a positive effect?

7. **Highlight strengths**.

Why is this important? Many ADHD children are so used to negative feedback that they do not realize that they really do have special strengths and skills. They need to know that what they have to offer the world is something positive as well as something that makes them special. If asked, ADHD children could produce a lengthy list of their weaknesses, but would find it very difficult to come up with even two or three strengths. That is so sad! Helping them find these strengths and build on them is essential to strong self-esteem

What can grandparents do to help?

- Mention special strengths when you see them and explain why these significant and unique. Let him hear you comment on his strengths to others.

- Produce an actual written list of these qualities. He will read this list over and over, I promise.

- Find ways to display these strengths. Hang up artwork, serve his cookies, or frame a difficult puzzle that he put together. When he sees that Grandma or Grandpa believes that he can do something that is wonderful enough to show or tell others about, his esteem and pride in his achievements are magnified.

8. **Provide opportunities for your child to help**.

   Why is this important? What a great feeling it is to know that they are the givers of help rather than always being the one who needs the help. We all feel good about ourselves when we have helped other people, and the ADHD children need to demonstrate their areas of strength. Completing a task and doing it well can make them feel good about themselves and take pride in their accomplishments—no matter what the undertaking.

   What can grandparents do to help?

   - Include him in charity work at a shelter or at your church. Helping someone else feels good and lets him know how useful he can be. It also builds a bond when you can share such meaningful work.

   - Give him chores that will have visible results to admire. Everyone can admire a table that has been set, a swept porch, or place cards at a family dinner.

   - Have him choose toys that he has outgrown. Together you can clean and repair them to donate to someone in need. Share stories of a time when you played with these together.

   - Give him responsibility to read or play with a younger child. If reading isn't a strength, have him 'teach' something to a younger child.

9. **Have realistic expectations and goals for your child.**

Why is this important? Your ADHD grandchildren need limits, just like every other child. If he is not held accountable for his behavior or he feels that he is not expected to behave because of ADHD, you are sending a message that he is not capable of good behavior or that you do not have any expectation that he can succeed. Setting and attaining goals is great for confidence building and the feeling of, "I can do this." If you know a child can sit still for only 15 minutes, don't expect him to sit still for an hour at his cousin's graduation ceremony. This only sets up a failure situation. He gets in trouble, his fiasco is public, and his parents feel inept in front of the whole family and everyone in the audience. When realistic goals are attained, however, it creates a feeling of empowerment and self-control for the ADHD child. In creating expectations and goals, grandparents have a special edge. We can probably give more time, and we seem to have more untapped patience where our grandchildren are concerned. What we lack in youth, we make up in appreciating and loving our grandchildren.

What can grandparents do to help?

- Purposely arrange a situation you know he can do successfully so you have a chance to point out this achievement. It can be simple like hanging up a coat or getting the newspaper from the front porch and taking it to Grandpa's desk.

- Plan ahead so you are able to provide appropriate activities that will help him control behavior. This might be a sticker or comic book in your purse, or a pre-selected quiet place for alone time where he can regroup.

- Set a goal together and provide the tools and support to reach the goal. For example:

  o See if you can stack all these magazines into piles. I can hand them to you and you stack them up by size.

  o The news will be on for ten more minutes. If you can watch this with me without interrupting for these ten minutes, I will be ready to play that game with you. While we watch, let's see if they show pictures of the President on the news.

10. **If your child has a learning disability, help your child to understand the nature of the problem.**

Why is this important? The more a child understands about his problem, the better able he is to ask for and receive the help he needs to advocate for his own success. When a child does not know the facts about his disability, he will tend to have misconceptions that are far worse than the truth! Many of the children I have tested are so relieved to hear exactly why they have been having academic problems. They had assumed they were just stupid and surely would never complete high school. Knowing the facts can give children hope, control of the situation, and direction toward the future. Understanding their weaknesses helps them learn to compensate and advocate. This is empowering.

Before discussing ADHD with your grandchild, be sure to ask the parents for permission to do so. Often, parents want to do this themselves, or they feel they are protecting their ADHD child by trying to hide it. This can be a big mistake. These children know that something is wrong. What our grandchildren do not know CAN hurt them; however, it is still the parents' decision.

What can grandparents do to help?

- Learn everything you can about ADHD to be a knowledgeable resource

- Let him know that ADHD children are intelligent— probably more intelligent than many of his classmates. Share the list of unique qualities found in many ADHD children.

- Express your confidence in his ability to succeed and share stories of successful ADHD adults.

- Ask him to explain his ADHD in his own words. This will be a great self- advocacy tool. Then ask him what kinds of things help with self-control, better behavior, or trying to learn hard things. Brainstorm these ideas and keep a list of what works well.

- Help him explore his strengths and expand on them during your special time together. It will provide a special bond to share and will demonstrate your belief that someday he might use this gift to do something memorable—just like the famous adults you talked about.

In summary:

- Strong self-esteem can mean the difference between success and failure in any child

- ADHD children have a tendency to judge themselves negatively and have lowered self-esteem.

- Adults can have a major impact on a child's self-esteem.

- Unconditional love and acceptance are essential in developing strong self-esteem.

- No one loves or accepts a child more openly or unconditionally than a grandparent!

Nobody can do for little children
what grandparents do.
Grandparents sort of sprinkle stardust over the lives
of little children.

~Alex Haley

Chapter XIII. Just in case you wanted more . . .

What you can do for yourself

1. Learn everything you can about ADHD. If grandparents are knowledgeable and positive, they can do a great deal in eliminating myths.

2. Let go of your old believes and prejudices about ADHD

3. Attend local speakers

4. Attend IEP (Individualized Education Program) meetings with your children if invited

5. Take care of yourself and continue activities that you love. You cannot be helpful to anyone else if you are not in your best way.

6. Prepare your home for relaxed visits.   Put away the breakables!

7. Share your feelings with others in your situation. Support groups like CHADD or Grandparent to Grandparent offer excellent resources.

8. Grieving is a normal reaction to hearing that your grandchild has any kind of problem.   Shock, sadness, blame, and disappointment are part of the grieving process, but keep these private. It's good to know that what you are feeling is predictable. Eventually you will feel acceptance and be an active part of the solution.

9. Think positive and remember all the famous successful people with ADHD.

What you can do for the ADHD grandchild

1. Remind yourself that he or she is a child first. This child happens to have ADHD.

2. Find the positive qualities and point them out.

3. Stay actively involved with your grandchild. Write letters or email, call, and consider getting an inexpensive web camera if you enjoy using your computer.

4. Be a cheer leader and praise small victories .

5. Provide a safe place and unconditional love.

6. Listen to the child, respect his feelings & don't interrupt. Hear with your heart.

7. Enjoy being a grandparent. Play, laugh, and be a kid again.

8. Observe and note weak social skills so you can rehearse appropriate alternative. These must be directly taught at a private time.

9. Find something special you can share and do with the grandchild. Make it a very personal relationship.

10. Watch for signs your grandchild has reached her limits so you can provide pleasant down time. Quiet music in a peaceful environment will avert a possible meltdown! Everyone feels better!

11. Studies indicate that a 20-minute outdoor experience goes a long way to improve concentration in ADHD children. Do it together!

12. Always have some diversions handy. Be able to pull out a book, a toy, or a DVD that can diffuse a behavior issue. Plan ahead for this.

13. Set aside some alone time with you to do things that your grandchild enjoys. Make sure there is no pressure and point out his successes. You might even want to make a written list for him to keep.

14. Model problem solving skills. Brainstorm solutions together. This is empowering and builds self esteem.

15. Be available for him, be a non-judgmental partner, and listen to him with your heart wide open.

16. Provide realistic goals. Don't expect him to sit perfectly still through an hour church service when his attention span lasts 12 minutes. Diversion time!

17. Let her know you understand her frustrations and feelings and are on her side. This does not mean rushing in to solve all problems or being overprotective.

What you can do for the siblings of the ADHD child

1. Give each grandchild special one-on-one time with you.

2. Listen to the sibling talk about the stresses he feels having an ADHD brother or sister. These are real, and he needs a place to vent safely. These usually involve jealousy, resentment, embarrassment, and guilt.

3. By listening with understanding, you can help deflect negative feelings. Listen and brainstorm without name-calling. Providing that sympathetic ear is more valuable than rushing in and making changes.

4. Try not to be overprotective of the ADHD child or the sibling will see it as favoritism.

5. Remind the sibling that all brothers and sisters fight. It's normal.

6. Answer the sibling's questions honestly. They need to be kept in the know.

7. Do not put all the pressure on the siblings to be the one that always has to give in or back down. Do not expect too much of the non-ADHD sib.

8. Provide opportunities to allow siblings to spend time alone with their parents.

9. Try to avoid competition when you are with the grandchildren. Provide group activities that require cooperation.

10. Keep chores even. Do not make the non-ADHD child do more. He is probably feeling over-worked and under-appreciated by his parents.

11. Remember that siblings deserve lives of their own.

12. Watch out for signs of perfectionism in the non-ADHD siblings. This might develop in their efforts to make life easier for their parents since they see the parents struggling with the 'imperfect' child.

13. If you see any signs that the non-ADHD child is being victimized by the ADHD child or is in any danger, take a stand. Bring this to the attention of the parents privately at an appropriate time. Describe what you saw.

What you can do for the parents of the ADHD child
Emotionally

1. Support them with praise that they are doing a good job.

2. Try to always remember that you are not the parent of the ADHD child; you are not calling the shots.

3. Do not compare grandchildren

4. Follow the parents' lead in all areas.

5. Be mindful of sharing private information with your bridge club. Respect the parents' right to privacy

6. Do not blame the parents for the ADHD.

7. Do not tell the parents there is no such thing or that they need to discipline better.

8. Respect the parents' decisions. This includes school, medication, or day-to-day family life.

9. Your adult child needs someone to talk to who will be supportive and understanding. He or she is constantly fighting battles for this ADHD child. Calling you should not feel like another challenge.

10. Tell them how much you love their child just the way she is. They don't hear that very often.

11. Do not be critical of teachers, doctors, and therapies in front of the child. In fact, it is not your place to voice these criticisms at all.

12. Be aware how tiring and stressful it is on parents to have an ADHD child. Keep giving them positive strokes. Parents are likely to be feeling inadequate in their parenting.

13. Remove potential stressors from your visits. Do not judge the meals that are served or the cleanliness of the home.

14. Be aware of the strain put on the marriage by having an ADHD child. Listen to the venting, but do not add fuel to the fire.

15. Stay loose and positive (at least on the outside!)

16. Learn all that you can about ADHD so you can dispel some of the myths and prejudices. Your adult children will love you for it.

17. Try to carry out the same schedules and rules so that the parents feel supported rather than undermined.

18. Apologize for giving unsolicited advice or butting in.

19. Discuss limits with the parents such as bedtime, foods, TV time, etc.

20. Celebrate all progress and give the parents credit.

Physically

1. Be available and willing

2. Offer to do things and do not wait to be asked.

3. Listen and do not interrupt or judge.

4. Take over some of the chores such as driving carpools, picking up dry cleaning, fixing too much dinner and sharing it with your daughter-in-law.

5. Offer to drive the child to the tutor

6. Give the parents a night out away from the kids. Baby-sit if you are able or provide a sitter.

7. Take the grandchild to your home, one at a time. Be sure to take the ADHD child now and then. Parents really need a break.

8. Attend meetings or go hear speakers on ADHD topics.

9. Give equal time to all the children.

10. Give parents some relief during outings. Take charge of watching the kids play for a while so the parents can enjoy the other adults without worry.

11. Let parents know that you are prepared for their visits. Breakables are put away, a private place is available for chilling out, and you've gotten calming distractions ready to go. What a pleasure to visit this grandmother!

12. Accompany parents to doctors' visits or other outings where another set of hands and eyes would be helpful.

13. Make a special night with the ADHD child so that the other siblings can enjoy a more carefree night with their parents.

Financially (Only if you can)

1. Treat your adult children to a night out

2. Help pay tuition to special schools.

3. Help pay for expensive tutoring

4. Purchase assistive technology that will benefit the ADHD child.

5. Send your grandchild to special activities that complement his strengths and interests. This could be special art lessons or tennis lessons. Encourage the strengths and positive activities.

6. Pay for summer camp opportunities for ADHD children. These often include much needed social skill training.

7. Help pay for your adult children to attend conferences and workshops about ADHD. In addition to excellent information, the chance to talk with peers about similar problems is so good for the soul.

8. If you cannot be the babysitter, pay for the babysitter.

9. Offer to pay for repairs or a cleaning crew without sounding like you are being critical.

21. Discuss limits with the parents such as bedtime, foods, TV time, etc.

22. Celebrate all progress and give the parents credit.

Notes

DSM-5 Criteria for ADHD

People with ADHD show a persistent pattern of inattention and/or hyperactivity-impulsivity that interferes with functioning or development:

1. **Inattention: Six or more symptoms of inattention for children up to age 16, or five or more for adolescents 17 and older and adults; symptoms of inattention have been present for at least 6 months, and they are inappropriate for developmental level:**
   o Often fails to give close attention to details or makes careless mistakes in schoolwork, at work, or with other activities.
   o Often has trouble holding attention on tasks or play activities.
   o Often does not seem to listen when spoken to directly.
   o Often does not follow through on instructions and fails to finish schoolwork, chores, or duties in the workplace (e.g., loses focus, side-tracked).
   o Often has trouble organizing tasks and activities.
   o Often avoids, dislikes, or is reluctant to do tasks that require mental effort over a long period of time (such as schoolwork or homework).
   o Often loses things necessary for tasks and activities (e.g. school materials, pencils, books, tools, wallets, keys, paperwork, eyeglasses, mobile telephones).
   o Is often easily distracted
   o Is often forgetful in daily activities.

2. **Hyperactivity and Impulsivity: Six or more symptoms of hyperactivity-impulsivity for**

children up to age 16, or five or more for adolescents 17 and older and adults; symptoms of hyperactivity-impulsivity have been **present for at least 6 months to an extent that is disruptive and inappropriate for the person's developmental level:**

- o Often fidgets with or taps hands or feet, or squirms in seat.
- o Often leaves seat in situations when remaining seated is expected.
- o Often runs about or climbs in situations where it is not appropriate (adolescents or adults may be limited to feeling restless).
- o Often unable to play or take part in leisure activities quietly.
- o Is often "on the go" acting as if "driven by a motor".
- o Often talks excessively.
- o Often blurts out an answer before a question has been completed.
- o Often has trouble waiting his/her turn.
- o Often interrupts or intrudes on others (e.g., butts into conversations or games)

In addition, the following conditions must be met:

- Several inattentive or hyperactive-impulsive symptoms were present before age 12 years.
- Several symptoms are present in two or more setting, (e.g., at home, school or work; with friends or relatives; in other activities).
- There is clear evidence that the symptoms interfere with, or reduce the quality of, social, school, or work functioning.
- The symptoms do not happen only during the course of schizophrenia or another psychotic disorder. The symptoms are not better explained by another mental disorder (e.g.

107

Mood Disorder, Anxiety Disorder, Dissociative
Disorder, or a Personality Disorder).

Based on the types of symptoms, three kinds (presentations) of ADHD can occur:

Combined Presentation: if enough symptoms of both
criteria *Presentation*: if enough symptoms of inattention,
but not hyperactivity-impulsivity, were present for the
inattention and hyperactivity-impulsivity were present for
the past 6 months
Predominantly Inattentive past six months
Predominantly Hyperactive-Impulsive Presentation: if
enough symptoms of hyperactivity-impulsivity but not
inattention were present for the past six months.
Because symptoms can change over time, the presentation
may change over time as well.

Reference

American Psychiatric Association: Diagnostic and Statistical
Manual of Mental Disorders, Fourth Edition, Text Revision.
Washington, DC, American Psychiatric Association, 2000.

Resources on ADHD and Grandparents of ADHD Children

Links

CHADD Children and Adults with Attention Deficit/Hyperactivity Disorder

8181 Professional Place, Suite 201

Landover, MD 20785

(800) 233-4050

www.chadd.org

ADDA Attention Deficit Disorder Association

1788 Second street, Suite 200

Highland Park, IL 60035

(847) 432-ADDA

http://www.add.org/

LDA Learning Disability Association of America

4156 Library Road

Pittsburgh, PA 15234

(412) 341-1515

www.ldanatl.org

LD Online

http://www.ldonline.org/

Support for Parents of ADHD on Facebook

https://www.facebook.com/ADD.ADHDSupport

AAN American Academy of Neurology

1080 Montreal Avenue

Saint Paul, MN 55116

(800) 879-1960

www.aan.com

AACAP American Academy of Child and Adolescent
Psychiatr

3615 Wisconsin Ave., N.W.

Washington, D.C. 20016-3007

(202) 966-7300

http://www.aacap.org/

National Center for Gender Issues and ADHD

1001 Spring Street, Suite 206

Silver Spring, MD 20910

(202) 966-1561

http://www.ncgiadd.org/

The Attention Deficit Information Network, Inc.

58 Prince Street

Needham, MA 02492

(781) 455-9895

www.addinfonetwork.com

U.S. Department of Education Office of Special

Education Programs

400 Maryland Ave., S.W.

Washington, DC 20202

(202) 205-5507

www.ed.gov/offices/OSERS/OSEP

When Your Grandchild Has ADHD

http://www.ncpamd.com/grandchildren.htm

The Gifted Child With ADHD

http://www.ncpamd.com/Gifted_ADD.htm

http://www.helpguide.org/mental/adhd_add_signs_sympt
oms.htm

http://www.myadhd.com/librarytools.html

http://www.myadhd.com/aboutadhd.html

Book Lists About ADHD

"Must Have" Books on ADHD at

http://www.healthyplace.com/adhd/books/must-have-books-on-children-and-adults-with-adhd/

All Kinds Of Minds:A Young Student's Book About Learning Abilities and Learning Disorders Mel Levine, M.D.

Driven To Distraction, Edward M Hallowell and John J. Ratey

The Self-Esteem Teacher, Robert Brooks

When You Worry About the Child You Love:Emotional and Learning Problems in Children, Edward M. Hallowell, M.D.

CHADD Booklist for Parents

http://www.amazon.com/My-ADHD-Book-List-Parents/lm/R3MSGF6EH4VBL3

Parenting Children with ADHD: 10 Lessons That Medicine Cannot Teach by Vincent Monastra

Superparenting for ADD: An Innovative Approach to Raising Your Distracted Child Edward Hallowell, MD.

You Mean I'm Not Lazy, Stupid or Crazy?!: The Classic Self-Help Book for Adults with Attention Deficit Disorder by Kate Kelly and Peggy Ramundo

Rick Lavoie's Books and Videos

The Motivation Breakthrough

It's So Much Work To Be Your Friend

How Difficult Can This Be? Fat City

Last One Picked, First One Picked On

Learning Disabilities and Discipline

http://www.ricklavoie.com/videos.html

Recommended Books on ADHD at Psych Central
http://psychcentral.com/lib/2008/recommended-books-on-adhd/

Index

ADD	1	Driven To Distraction	60
ADDA	109	Edison, Thomas	72
American Psychiatric Association	15	Einstein, Albert	73
American with Disabilities Act	9	Family gatherings	47-50
Andries, Darcy	63,64	Fear	38,42
Attention Deficit Information Network	111	Frost, Robert	73
Aunts and Uncles	47,49	Girls and ADHD	13
Barkley, Russell	9	Goldberg, Whoopie	74
Cannell, Stephen	74	Guilt	37,79
CHADD	77, 109	Hallowell, Edward	60,79
Cher	76	Hereditary	2
Christie, Agatha	73	Hilfiger, Tommy	74
Churchill,Winston	73	Hopkins, Anthony	75
Conversation	54-57	Hyperactive	3,10,14
Coordinated Campaign for Learning Disabilities	82	IEP	95
Department of Education	9	Impulsive	3, 52,108
Devalued	38	Inattentive	2,3,53, 106

Individuals with Disabilities Act	9	Pragmatic Language	54
Intelligence	11	Ratey, John	60,113
Intimacy	29	Ritalin	12
It's So Much Work To Be Your Friend	54	Sarcasm	49,55
Jealousy	36	Self-esteem	8,29,82
Kinko's	77	Shaywitz, Sally	78
Lavoie, Richard	24,54.114	Siblings	35-40, 53, 98
Learning Disability Association	109	Social Success	54
Marriage problems	25-34	Stress Producer	20-22
Meckler, Alan	79	Stress Reducer	20-22
Money strain	27,103	U.S. Dept. of Education	9
National Institute of Health	9	Vedantan, Shankar	25
Neeleman, David	78	Winkler, Henry	75
Newton, Sir Isaac	70	www.suite101.com	63
Office of Civil Rights	9		
On The Waterbed	23-24		
Orfalea, Paul	77,78		
Phelps, Michael	77		
Positive side o ADHD	59-64,78		

Everyone needs to have access
both to grandparents and grandchildren
in order to be a full human being.
~Margaret Mead

ABOUT THE AUTHOR

Judy Kirzner is a National Board Certified Teacher, Exceptional Needs Specialist, with more than twenty-five years of classroom experience in both public and private schools. In addition, she has a master of education degree and is a reading specialist, and served as her school's instructional specialist and case manager for students with learning disabilities and Attention Deficit Hyperactive Disorder. Judy is a consultant on technology for learning disabled students, and has been a lecturer and advisor on best colleges for ADHD students. Most importantly, Judy is a grandparent.

CPSIA information can be obtained
at www.ICGtesting.com
Printed in the USA
FSOW03n1110220617
35527FS